A HILARIOUS PARODY BOOK ABOUT PREGNANCY, EARLY PARENTING, AND TOTAL ~~CHAOS~~ BLISS

PURE BLISS

Written by
MADELINE SHEPPARD

Illustrated by
RACHEL DUROCHER

PURE BLISS

A hilarious parody book about pregnancy, early parenting, and total ~~chaos~~ bliss

Illustrations - Rachel Durocher
Cover Design - LeadHer Publishing
Editing - Courtney St Croix
ISBN Paperback - 978-1-998411-32-0

leadher
PUBLISHING

DEDICATION

Dedicated to our kids, who gave us all
the inspiration, and to all the parents
out there, currently in the trenches.

We see you, and we're right
there with you.

T'was a family gathering, pure friggin' delight,
Toddlers were shrieking, and dogs picked a fight.
The stool was unstable, the pasta half-cooked,
A kid flushed the car keys and gave a proud look.

In the midst of the mess, my husband found peace,
Looked up with a grin and whispered,
"It's Bliss...pure bliss...my sweet!" *wink*

And thus, it was born: our new family creed,
When sh*t hits the fan, this is all that you need:

PURE BLISSSSSSSSSS.

So... what is Pure Bliss? Want the real, honest scoop?
It's being knee-deep in laundry, toads in your slippers, and poop.

It's sleepless nights and a toddler who stares,
Covered in glitter. Mid-air. On the stairs.

It's crying while laughing.
It's rage mixed with love.

It's googling "WhY dOes mY tOdDleR eAt bUgS!?!?"

"Close your eyes, breathe deep, in this chaotic abyss,
say it with pride now: PURE FRIKEN BLISS.

Three trimesters of magic? More like three acts of war.
Your body's possessed, and then there's the snore.

Do you pee when you sneeze? Do your curtains smell weird?
Has your partner breathed wrong, and has your patience disappeared?

Are you puking at red lights? Do smells make you rage?
Does meat make you gag? Are you riding the hormonal rampage?

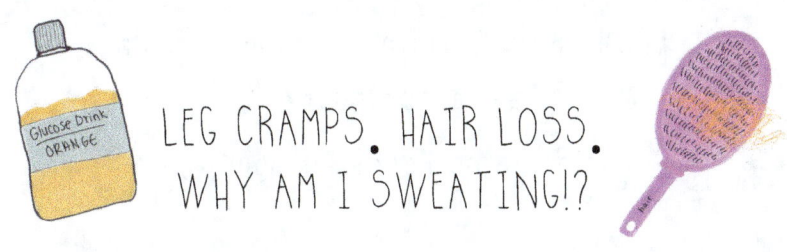

LEG CRAMPS. HAIR LOSS.
WHY AM I SWEATING!?

And don't get me started on the glucose test dreading.
Bar skills apply as you chug that sweet drink,
and try not to vomit in the waiting room sink.

I trained for this in 2012,
but now it's glucose, not Grey Goose, I fear.
Muscle memory is strong, and the target is clear.

Oh, and let's not forget this one last little twist:
They call it morning sickness, but it's

ALL DAY BULLSH*T!!!

PURE NAUSEOUS BLISS!

4

The blissful hospital check-in is here!
You're contracting?

(Hold on, he needs his gear...)

Where's the Charger!?

My Hat...?

Where are my snacks ????

do I need a pillow?

You're screaming in pain. He's calm as can be (!?)
This man packed slippers and snacks...but not for ME?!?!

PURE EFFIN' BLISS

You made it home, hooray! Welcome back!
Now flaunt that sexy vag ice pack.

The boobs leak, the blowouts, the guilt creeps in,
and right on cue, the visitors drop in.
You're crying in corners while you fake a grin.

"When are you going back to work?"

You're juggling feeds, wake windows, naps, and tracking it all.
Packing a suitcase just to go to the mall.

You're leaking and weeping, you're sad and you're
pissed, But say it! Say it again now:

PURE FREAKING BLISS!

"Did your baby sleep!?" Oh, screw you, pal.
Mine's up every hour, making me howl.

You've tried it all: white noise, sleep sacks, the rest...
Your baby still thinks naps are a punishment at best.

shhh...

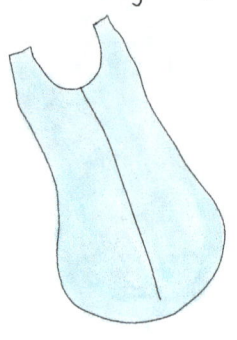 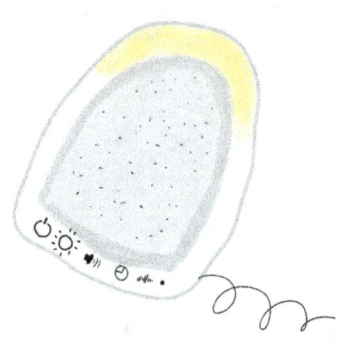

You're a mombi now. With wine and despair.
Dark circles, no pants, and unwashed hair.

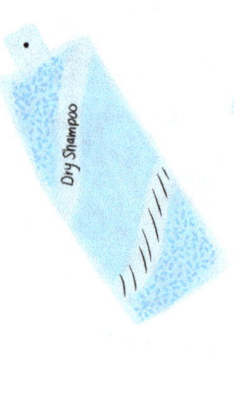

PURE

HOW

AM I

ALIVE?!?!

BLISS

r.i.p

sleep + sanity

beware of mombies...

Tummy time, then bouncy chair,
a blowout up to the baby's hair.

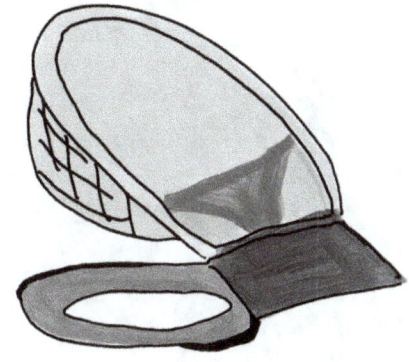

Snack attack, then spit-up rain,
welcome to the baby train!

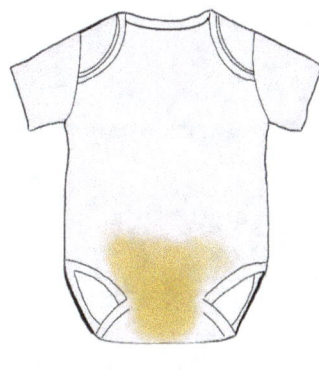

pure

why don't mustard
stains come out?

blisssssss!

Yogurt tsunami, a splash with no shame.

The high chair straps?
Oh they'll never be the same.

Spoon hits the floor, then comes the roar,
meal time's a sport I did not train for.

PURE *ScRub-TiL-yOu-DrOp* BLISS

Now, get your game face on — 5,4,3,2,1. All systems GO!

The bedtime routine is a performance of art,
where science meets madness and breaks every heart.

The bath, the lotion, the PJs, the book,
the last little cuddle, and the last little look.

Then comes the drop into the crib, gently placed.
DON'T MAKE A SOUND!!! (Or you'll restart this whole chase!)

Bare sweaty feet? That squeak of the floor?

Oh, no! You're done. You're toast.

Reset it once more. *Sigh*

Then finally...

...silence.

You sit in the gloom. → Nobody move. Nobody speak.
Wine in your hand. Alone in the room. ∫ We've found bliss in this wine-sipping technique.

PURE SILENT BLISS

You're changing inside. People get weird.
You're softer, you're stronger, you've cried and you've cheered.

You've lost your pink, but that's okay.
You'll find her again on another day.

PURE ~eVoLVinG aS a wOmAn~ BLISS

Wait, crap...how did we almost forget...(we may still be recovering)

They walk, they dump, they chew, (Oh! Do they chew!!!)
Everything goes into their mouths, nothing's safe, it's true!!!
The REMOTE, their SHOES, DIRT and ROCKS too!

They climb, they launch, they vanish, they run.
From sunrise to bedtime, they are never done.

They scale the couch, the table, the log -
always in motion, like a caffeinated frog.

Who's having fun?

We BEGGED for steps!!!

WHAT WERE WE THINKING?!

Pure "please don't invite us over" bliss

READY...
SET...
GOOOO!!!

15

Here come the little dictators! CHAOS AHEAD!
In rain boots only. Naked but fed.

They run, they climb, they headbutt walls,
they empty the fridge and smear boogers down the halls.

PURE BLISSY BLISS!

We baby-proofed the kitchen, the bathroom, the hall,
put gates up so high they resembled a wall.

But our toddler's a ninja, he scaled with such grace,
now the living room is his training base.

He escaped from his crib at just 14 months,
unlocked every door like he's solving a hunt.

We bolt every handle, we plan and prepare...
Yet he climbs like a squirrel and flies through the air.

PURE  BLISS

Wanna know a secret?

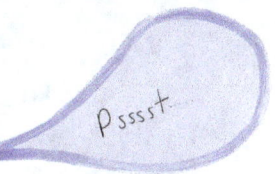

Pssst.

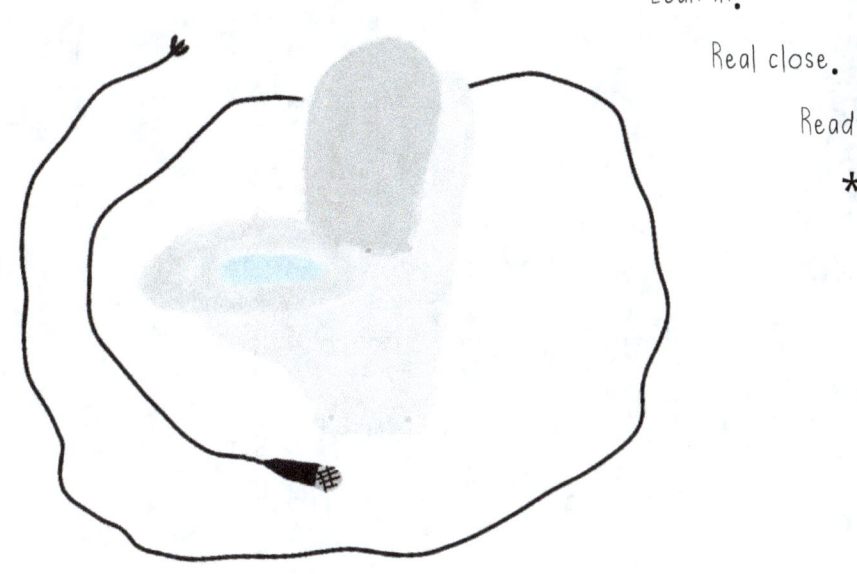

Lean in.

Real close.

Ready?

whispers

You're

never

gonna

be

alone

again.

(sorry!)

Tiny feet slap down the hall,
now they're beside you, licking the wall.

Doors? Useless. Locks? A joke.
You now pee under supervision, folks.

As tiny lungs unleash their might,
in bathroom concerts, day and night.

pure supervised bliss

There's a new word you'll hear,
they'll yell it out loud,
you'll fake a small smile,
and nod to the crowd.

Have you guessed it?
Say it with me now...

19

POOP!
POOP!
POOP!

Oh yes!!!
Poopy mom. Poopy dad.

Poopy tree.

Poopy dinosaur drinking poopy tea.

"Mmm!"

Poopy clouds.
Poopy car.
Poopy sun.

Everything's poop. Isn't this fun?

(We have no idea when this fun ends,
we'll get back to you on that...)

Dressing a toddler? Oh you mean an alligator fight?
They bite, they roll, they vanish from sight.

One sock on and one off - total outrage!
It's a circus meets boot camp on a living room stage.

You whisper, "We did it." They poop...scene change.

PURE JESUS TAKE THE WHEEL BLISS

Wait – before you leave, check the map of their soul.
The monster truck must sit inside the cereal bowl.

Banana on stairs, Yoda on chair,
and the marble must live in the dragon's lair.

You move one item? They'll burn it all down.
This is pure bliss...
With a toddler crown.

You brought all the snacks, the sippy cups, the gear...
Yet forgot your dignity. It's not welcome here.
You'll wrestle them into a change room door,
and cry as they sprint through the grocery store.

The joy of leaving the house with your crew,
a bliss club field trip (what could go askew?).

Oh wait - not joyous, that part was amiss.
It's chaos and parking lot meltdowns.

did I Brush
my teeth?

do I have
deodorant on?!?

It's pure sweaty bliss!

Congrats!

You've unlocked a new level of pain.
THE "I DO IT!" PHASE

...and it's not very sane

How dare you help.
How dare you breathe.
How dare you buckle the car seat with ease.

Just smile through the madness, that's all you can do.
While a tiny dictator throws shoes at you.

PURE SURVIVAL BLISS

(Hey! Yes you...psst...before we move on?)

Toddler parents y'all good? You still alive?
These feral animals just barely let us survive.

You got This...

Barely...

You're doing a great job, even when they're loud.
Even when they flash strangers and yell "the poop is out" in a crowd.

Beware the couch. The moment you sit...

You'll hear "SNACT!" and just like that...!

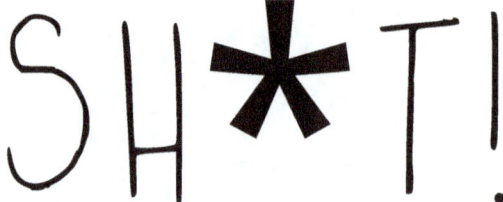

They want a snack. A weird snack.

A snack from the moon.

And they want it served now.

Or you meet your doom.

PURE NEVER SIT DOWN BLISS

To you, tired heroes, we see what you do.
This mess, this madness... we're right here with you!

The day's been a blur. You sit down and sigh.
They're finally asleep and you want to cry.

It's okay to daydream of running away.
You'll come back by dinner...
(it's not a long-term stray!)

It's hard. It's brutal. It's love on fire.
But we'll persist and survive... with humour and satire.

Laugh through the tears, dance through the stress,
welcome to the club of Pure Effing Bliss.

We love them so much. It's okay that it's hard.
One day, you'll poop in peace and drive a clean car.

YOU ARE SEEN. YOU ARE ENOUGH. YOU GOT THIS.

The world might miss it,
but we know you're doing the hardest work there is.

With love,
from us to you!

Madeline   Rachel

(P.S. We'll be back with even more,
buckle up for the next stage of bliss....)

32

ABOUT THE AUTHORS

MADELINE SHEPPARD is a former competitive figure skater turned coach, now raising two wild and wonderful boys with her husband Dan on the scenic west coast of Newfoundland. As a passionate advocate for early childhood education and a lover of adventure, Madeline brings energy, humour, and heart to everything she does. The chaos of motherhood inspired her to co-create this playful, honest look at parenting. Her hope is that fellow parents laugh, relate, and feel a little less alone.

RACHEL DUROCHER is a stay-at-home mom of two, raising her family in small-town Muskoka with her husband, Hayden. With a background in hospitality and a love for books, baking sourdough, skiing, and dabbling in pottery, Rachel finds joy in the messy, beautiful chaos of everyday life. Writing this book felt like the perfect way to connect with other parents who are deep "in the thick of it." Her goal is to make you laugh, nod in solidarity, and feel seen and validated.

Connect with Madeline and Rachel!

📷 @pureblissbook   📘 Pure Bliss   ✉️ pureblissbook@gmail.com

Leave us a review!

If you enjoyed reading Pure Bliss, consider leaving a 5 star ranking and review on Amazon! Positive reviews help the book get into the hands of more readers like you!

www.ingramcontent.com/pod-product-compliance
Lightning Source LLC
Chambersburg PA
CBHW081012120626
46546CB00010B/3115

* 9 7 8 1 9 9 8 4 1 1 3 2 0 *